Build Your Empire

OTHER BOOKS BY THE AUTHOR

The Five Enemies (Self-Help, Spiritual, 2006)

Build Your Empire

A Guide and Workbook for Entrepreneures

Daphne K. McCorery

iUniverse, Inc.

New York Lincoln Shanghai

Build Your Empire
A Guide and Workbook for Entrepreneures

iUniverse books may be ordered through booksellers or by contacting:

iUniverse
2021 Pine Lake Road, Suite 100
Lincoln, NE 68512
www.iuniverse.com
1-800-Authors (1-800-288-4677)

Because of the dynamic nature of the Internet, any Web addresses or links contained in this book may have changed since publication and may no longer be valid.

The information, ideas, and suggestions in this book are not intended to render professional advice. Before following any suggestions contained in this book, you should consult your personal accountant or other financial advisor. Neither the author nor the publisher shall be liable or responsible for any loss or damage allegedly arising as a consequence of your use or application of any information or suggestions in this book.

New, Expanded, Revised Edition

ISBN: 978-0-595-46442-5 (pbk)
ISBN: 978-0-595-90738-0 (ebk)

Printed in the United States of America

Contents

SECTION TWO Business Tool Box Workbook

Preface

"Plan for prosperity not retirement. Enjoy your life now."

You are probably well aware that a college education and job are no longer the key to a prosperous future.

The cost of living today is so high many people feel they never have enough money.

When I first realized my day job just wasn't going to make me rich, I started looking at the rich more closely. I had a few friends in high places and picked their brains a little. I enrolled in a small business certificate program, attended financial workshops, read books, and watched The Apprentice every week.

To have knowledge, however, is not enough. One must take action. This book is the result of that action. I'm happy to present you with a bigger, better, new, and expanded version of Build Your Empire: A Guide and Workbook for Entrepreneurs.

After you read it, you'll have the ammunition you need to become richer than you are now. This edition is all about financial mastery and raising prosperity thinking in order to become financially literate and free.

Over the last three years I have researched more financial strategies, tips, and insight on how to improve your thinking to help you get rich. This version will definitely give you more bang for your bucks.

Some of the information I mentioned in the first version of this book (which was a mere 49 pages) has been deleted, rearranged, and revised.

When I published the book back in 2004, the main agenda was simply to fulfill one of my ultimate dreams: to write a book and contribute something of value to the planet.

I had wanted to write a book since the age of eighteen and ended up writing screenplays instead. The task of writing a book just seemed too great, too big of a dream back then.

However, as the years went by, the information I gathered and stored in my mind was ready to be expressed in the form of a book. All that work was about to pay off. I finally had a purpose for all that people watching and avid reading—especially in the area of self-help and money.

Another secret reason behind the creation of the book was to launch a new stream of income for myself. Unbeknownst to my friends, several of them criticized me for writing a book about something they perceived me not to be. Because I was not yet "super rich" in their eyes I had no business writing a book about building an empire.

One of them even had the nerve to ask me to explain what exactly made me an authority on the subject?

I told him *my life* made me an authority.

I grew up in a home of money troubles. My mother was equity rich, but cash poor.

I spent many years trying to understand money and uncover how it made people rich. I was on a mission to learn as much about how people got rich so there could be no more excuses when it came down to being plagued with money problems

Everyone jumped to conclusions without knowing the whole story. None of them knew my financial situation in intimate detail and still do not. Secondly, I knew I had the right to write a book on any subject I wanted. In fact, I went on to write a spiritual book and plan to write a book on relationships, too.

Ironically, poverty taught me better money management skills, opened up the world of investing and unlocked the mystery of how to start businesses from the ground up.

It made sense for me to write a book about money because I also had a history of engaging in various entrepreneurial activities.

When I was a little girl I never saw myself as a person who would someday work for others. I thought I was going to work for myself as an independent artist, but my mother destroyed those plans when she forced my siblings and me to work at an early age much against our will. Before I knew it, I was caught up in the 9 to 5 rat race at the age of 16 like many people and found it hard to escape and do my homework. Mind you, I started doing a lot of odd jobs at age eleven.

In spite of everything, I have always maintained an entrepreneurial spirit, yet I wasn't living my life like one. Eventually this lead to a much splintered life which I'll talk about more later.

What Exactly Is An Empire?

In my opinion, it is when material and spiritual well being meet and produce the absolute best results a person or group of people set out to accomplish.

The most important thing to remember is an empire can be large or small. It's about whatever you're comfortable with.

Like I said before, one or two million in net worth is good enough for me. This may not be enough for another person who is seeking 10, 20, or 30 million.

With that said, I am really excited about the changes in this book. I hope you enjoy it as much as I did writing it. I hope you walk away with a sense of enlightenment and belief in yourself that you can build an empire of any size once you commit yourself to it.

—Daphne K McCorery
May 23, 2007

Introduction:
The Major Streams Of Income

It was brought to my attention long ago that most people are not familiar with all the major streams of income.

For centuries the average citizen was a slave (and still is) to the **earned income stream**. When the rich of America introduced the Corporation the **paper income stream** was born and only they understood how to manage and operate the many complex nuances of the corporate structure.

The income stream that has evaded us all, the one that can make you rich beyond your wildest dreams primarily because it allows cash to flow without limitations and demands little to no physical exertion on the part of anyone, is known as the **residual or unearned income stream.**

Residual income is what we all should be aiming for. The following is a list of several ways passive income can be utilized. You do not have to have any special degrees or a high IQ to take advantage of them.

1. Interest
2. Royalties
3. Dividends
4. Equity
5. Rentals

The amount of income one yields depends on what one knows and how to go after it.

More and more people are beginning to explore one or two of these streams in addition to their earned income stream.

Some people know where to put their money to earn 16% APR on their money … some only get 1-2% on theirs.

Two landlords may both generate positive cash flow from duplex properties, but deal with very different operating costs each month. One may earn less or more than the other. The numbers depend on the market rent, mortgage, and other factors.

This book will address each stream of income in more detail in the chapters to come.

If you learn to take advantage of all three of these streams, you will gain financial mastery over your money.

No longer will you have to struggle with earned income which is "capped" and takes two weeks to earn before it is deposited into your bank accounts.

If money has caused too many problems in your life in the past, worry no more. With multiple streams of income flowing into your life, the stress of dealing with never having enough money will disappear. This I promise.

Quick Tips from the Millionaire Inside, CNBC

- Buy your retirement/vacation home early
- Look at stocks as a business.
- Buy businesses on sale.
- Don't reinvent the wheel.

SECTION ONE
33 Strategies, Tips, and Insight on How to Make You Rich

#1 You'll Never Be Successful If You Do Not Love What You Do

I would like to open this book with this very wise and thought provoking statement.

Look at your life.

Do you wake up in the morning and look forward to going to work?

A yes answer means you must have passion for what you do. If your work doesn't inspire you, you might get caught up in resentment, accepting whatever comes your way, and it will feel like something is planning your life for you. So make sure you pursue what you really love.

Why is this so important?

Because "you'll never be successful if you do not love what you do." Loving what you do lays down the foundation for stability and success.

I learned a lot from this profound statement uttered from the mouth of Donald Trump himself.

Keeping these words of wisdom in mind can release you from a life of never ending drudgery—especially if you have a habit of job hopping. Job hoppers have been accused of having ADD and needing variety in their work. They get bored easily.

Job hoppers, on the other hand, believe their jobs never mesh with their more creative side or personality.

Being aware of these words of wisdom can help you make the conscious choice to never, ever, look at another crappy job lead again.

Ever since I heard those wise words I have trained my mind to seek out only the things I enjoy. It has become easier to keep my eye on the prize.

In the past, I sometimes lacked focus and everyone influenced me. Before I knew it, I was stuck in work situations I despised and created long and hard unnecessary strife to get out of those situations.

The well balanced person loves what he or she does for a living. He or she does not waste energy dabbling in things that are not suitable.

Many of us feel we have no choice in most matters. We always feel we *have to* do what we are doing.

Try to exercise your right to do what you love.

Indulge in your passion.

Control what direction your life takes.

#2 The Power of a Decision

Have you ever hesitated to make a decision?

Are you fearful of what your choices might bring?

Making decisions is the best way to exercise power over your life. The minute you commit to a decision your life will change within that very moment you make that decision?

This is the inherit surprise that lies in making a decision.

If you do not believe me, make a decision right now and commit to it. Tell yourself you are going to make it happen. Can you feel the change taking place right now? Change doesn't have to take forever.

If you are planning to get rich, your decisions will have to reflect a bigger way of thinking. They will have to gravitate to the BBD—bigger, better deal. You cannot be plagued by a poor man's way of thinking.

The poor man's way of thinking or "poverty mindset" has held many people back. It held back our parents. It held back our friends. It held us back, too.

The Poverty Mindset thinks:

Money is the root of all evil
Feels guilty about money
Blames problems on money
Thinks small

Cannot Expand
Lacks Hopes
Refuses to learn and grow
Is fearful of taking risks
Remains caught in negativity

Thus pay close attention to the thoughts behind your decision. Are your thoughts filled with confidence? Do they excite you? Do they reflect where you want to go?

This is very important to remember. Your decision should take you where you want to be. The reason why decisions sometimes take us down roads we do not want to go is because they consist of mixed messages.

A rock solid decision reflects one message. It has been deeply analyzed and then is carried out as best as possible.

There are no conflicting thoughts or desires stirring from within.

Also know it's okay to altar your decisions or even abandon them all together if they do not serve you the way we originally thought. This is not giving up or failure. You can change your mind anytime and try another approach. The bottom line is to learn to make clear and fast decisions. Do not sit on the fence and watch your life go by. Do not fear the consequences either. If you do not venture, you will not gain.

#3 Check Your Action Steps Everyday

Reprogram your mind to see goals as action steps. When I first did this, I became more engaged with them. I no longer just wrote them down and put them away in my drawer to look again at a later date.

Action step thinking pushes you to take action. Action steps are more fun to work with.

You will feel compelled to check them daily to actually see if you are staying on track.

There's nothing like putting a line through an action step on a daily basis and seeing yourself getting closer and closer to actualizing your vision.

A goal now viewed as an action step may have seemed unattainable last year, but is not anymore. Now you're just a day away from success. You worked hard. You stuck to the plan. You broke down the goal into interactive steps.

Write your action steps down in a yearly planner and check them two, three, or even four times a day everyday.

Make adjustments as needed. If you neglect a step make sure to bring it forward and include it in next week's schedule.

This will take a bit of discipline. However, once you do this for one month, checking three or four times a day will become second nature.

It may even become your next obsession.

#4 Focus On The Outcome

Isn't it funny how we get carried away sometimes with details … little stuff … instead of the end product?

No wonder we tend to stay in one place. This piece of advice was brought to my attention through a conversation with my sister.

My sister and I remember spending too much on the little stuff when we were younger, forgetting to take a few minutes per day to visualize the bigger picture.

Just recently a local artist in my city launched an art exhibit online. He worked on the collection of art after work and on the weekends. Although he managed to get an article in the newspaper, he realized after the exhibit ended with poor results, he fretted so much over the presentation of art, the publicity suffered.

Making the art was easy. Getting the word out which would lead to sells and a donation to an organization was the hard part yet was not treated with priority. After all, this was the outcome he anticipated.

Sometimes working on details can derail us. We can forget the purpose of our plans. Know ahead of time where you are going and determine what you must do to reach the end.

Some people say they work backwards or start from the outcome. In other words, determine what you want your outcome to be and then write your action steps from the outcome to the first step.

So let's back up and look at the artist again. If he had started from the outcome which was to make sure he contacted maybe 100 newspapers instead of
one or two, he would have worked harder on promotions. Creating the art
would have been the least of his worries since creating art was the easiest tasks
for him to do.

#5 Try ... try ... try Again

Were you one of those kids whose parents and teachers pushed you to do something over and over again until you got it right? They just refused to let you give up?

Treating kids like this sometimes backfires and they become adults who never want to try anything more than once. No one stopped to consider that perhaps the method or approach was what kept their kids from breaking through the barriers.

When I look back on my life and count how many times I've had to do so many things over and over again, I get exhausted.

While caught up in my frustration I didn't realize how often I tackled a project in the same manner.

It's important that we keep trying until getting the results we want, but change our strategies.

Motivational speaker, Anthony Robbins, says there is no such thing as failure, only results. So the only way to produce the results you want is to keep trying.

Try until you succeed.

If you repeat the old way of doing things you will be destined to go around in circles.

I have watched several people in my life perfect what they do, experimenting with new mediums and methods over the course of many years. Some have reached the zenith of skill and presentation. In other words, they have reached their peak.

Until you feel a sense of elation, complete satisfaction, and receive your just rewards, you'll just have to keep trying.

Whenever you burn out, take a break. Recoup your energy. Revise your method. Then start again.

#6 Pay Yourself First

The "Pay Yourself First" concept, introduced by financial guru, Suze Orman, is already a popular way to build net worth. Even author, David Bach, constantly reminds the American public to always pay themselves first every time they get paid.

So there really is no need for me to talk about it. I just placed it in the book because it's very good advice. And who knows, you might just be hearing about it for the first time and I don't want to take any chances on not mentioning it.

After all, this book is all about good advice, and I've been a die hard "Pay Myself First" candidate for several years now.

Paying yourself first will test your discipline for saving money and money management as well.

It's easy to do. Tell everyone you know.

Before you know it or they realize it, everyone's bank account may have grown into a little fortune.

Speaking of fortune....

7 Open An Orange or Etrade Savings Account

The Orange Savings Account and E*TRADE wants to make you a fortune, too.

I want everyone to open one of these accounts today and then close those pathetically low interest paying Bank of America or Wells Fargo checking and savings accounts.

I opened an orange savings account on August 28, 2006. It has earned more interest in less than six months than my 1-2% credit union account has earned in one year. I have a third account at a conventional bank which hasn't impressed me much either.

One thing I will never understand are the incredibly low interest rates conventional banks offer compared to most European nations. It seems like a game of usury when a customer is tied to astronomical mortgage or credit card rates that take ten or more years to pay off. By the time the customer pays off the loan or line of credit, they have paid nearly double what they borrowed? Yet they can only offer us 0.57% to 2% to use the money in our savings accounts.

I call that a major a rip off!

Americans have not seen the value in saving their money until now.

According to Ing Direct's customer newsletter (April, 2007), customers have received as much as $4,570,015,953 in paid interest.

Ing Direct offers many other types of products including IRSs, home loans, and CD's. They even gave away a $25k 24-month Orange CD which was the grand prize in the Automatic Savings Plan Contest which ended January, 2007.

The orange savings account yield has stabilized at 4.50% APY. Take a look at what a bonus can do for you over a 10 year period:

Your Bonus	10 years later at 4.50% APY
$500	$776.47
$2,000	$3,105.95
$10,000	$15,529.64

The orange savings account is one of two of the best on the market in America today and is worth taking advantage of. Visit their website at www.ingdirect. com or call 1-888-464-7868.

Tip: E*TRADE offers savings account at 5.05% APY, more than 8x the national average which is 0.57%.. It's even higher than Ing.

#8 Create A Product

Have you ever had an idea for a new product? Many people are experts at something and can easily package their expertise as a product. Several things usually standing in their way may be a deep seated fear of taking a chance, money, or they are just completely unaware of the power they have in themselves to create a product that could bring them a windfall.

For example, I knew a massage therapist who created exotic bath teas based on formulas she learned in Hawaii for clients. I always thought her bath teas would fly off the shelves if she consulted with a manufacturer to help her package and distribute the product.

I think there are as many ideas out there as there are people. Almost anything goes.

Every day thousands of people around the world visit shopping malls.

A public speaker can record speeches on CD and distribute them in stores. The girl next door who paints landscapes can license the designs on table mats or journals.

Putting a new twist on existing products and making them "user friendlier" can sell like hot cakes if marketed well.

Creating a product may take a little bit of imagination? It may take a while to perfect. However, once you take have tested it and advertised it on QVC or HSN, the sky's the limit.

I suggested in the first version of this book to look at two things that work together such as a broom and dustpan and try to design a new way those two items could work as one in a more efficient way, creating a breakthrough gadget every household would have to have. A few weeks ago an engineer student introduced a new alarm clock on *The Big Idea* that jumps off the table and rolls around the floor when the snooze button is used. It forces people to get out of the bed if they wish to turn it off. Ingenious!!

I also mentioned several ways to obtain professional and monetary assistance for new product ideas.

Everyday thousands of people around the world visit shopping malls to purchase products from garden art to toys and electronics, never fully realizing these items are owned by regular folks who live next door.

I want you to pay close attention to this chapter because the products and invention market is an extremely coveted way a creative entrepreneurial individual can make big money and start building his or her empire.

When you deal with products verses service oriented businesses, you will discover that products can generate millions of dollars in a matter of minutes. For example a business owner who designs and sells a million dog leashes for $5 each will greatly surpass the owner of a dog walking service that walks several dogs for a flat rate of $500 per week.

If you want to make big money fast, choosing between a product or service business is a "no brainer." It's like the difference between renting and home-ownership. Homeowners build equity. Renters just pay their landlord's mortgage.

In order to play the products and inventions game requires a strong ability to create and materialize whatever we can imagine. We all can channel inspiration through visiting stores, talking to consumers to find out what they want, or trying to figure out a way to make an existing product more efficient and user-friendly.

Some products are carefully thought out while others are discovered by accident. *Airborne* was created by a school teacher who worked around small children and was constantly plagued by frequent colds she caught from the children. She began developing an herbal remedy at home to help fight the colds which eventually became the formula for Airborne. Before she knew it, Airborne was sold in hundreds of drugstores across the United States.

She is now a multi-millionaire.

There are several ways to obtain professional and monetary assistance for your product idea. Unit pricing is the beauty behind rapidly explosive brand empires. If one thousand units of a product priced at $24 are sold per day in five stores, the total units sold equal $24,000. Multiply $24,000 to 365 days per year, and you've just got paid big time. Yesterday I watched the Philosophy cosmetic line on QVC sell over 150,000 products within minutes. Some of the products were priced fewer than fifty dollars and some over fifty dollars. It was mind-blowing, and I'm sure the CEO of Philosophy was laughing all the way to the bank.

I'm going to illustrate the strategic steps you will need to implement in order to promote your product idea. Let's pretend you designed a very unique line of greeting cards. The artwork is whimsical and colorful and friends and family have responded favorably to them. How should you market the line? What are your choices? Well, there are typically three popular methods to marketing products. The first one is the best way to handle a greeting card line.

1.   Arrrange a license agreement where you (the client) receives an advance and percentage of profit known as royalties (usually 5%) from the sell of the cards. When a company licenses the cards, they agree to do the manufacturing, the distribution, the marketing and advertising at no cost to the client.

2.   The Direct Response industry has $30 Billion worth of advertising time left unsold each year that companies use to do zero cost media joint ventures. These companies are on the constant look out for merchandise to promote in many different ways. They pay the media a percentage of the sales they generate in exchange for advertising. A project, service, business opportunity and even website can be promoted or sold as a television infomercial, in a catalog, on the air via radio, through direct mail or as a television commercial.

QVC and the Home Shopping Network buy products in wholesale quantities such as toys at an agreed upon price. This is a type of joint venture.

3. There is also a joint venture known as "per inquiry" or "per order" which is self-explanatory. The media supplies exposure at no cost to the client; however, the client agrees to pay the media generally 25% of the retail price or 25% of the net profit.

Products and inventions with consumer appeal can put millions in your bank account. It is the perfect vehicle for a person who doesn't want to risk his or her money. Companies are always in need of new ideas and they will supply finance and develop your idea if they believe it will make millions.

Here is a brief list of products marketed through the avenues mentioned above:

1. Tony Robbin's Personal Power

2. George Forman's Grill

3. Taebo

4. Magic Mop

5. Bare Minerals

6. Carleton Sheets

#9 Generate Royalties

Do you want to create a stream of income that can take care of you for life?

If you have rights to a product or brand and want to find other ways to make it make more money for you, then listen up.

Consider licensing/endorsing products and services.

Most product endorsements have historically remained exclusive to celebrities. In fact this type of arrangement is called celebrity licensing. **An endorsement is a written or verbal pitch made by a celebrity to help launch products. This pitch is referred to as a" sales pitch "when applying to an ordinary citizen.** Donald Trump is no leading fashion designer, yet he markets a men's clothing line in his name for an upfront fee and future royalties as does dozen of other celebrities. His line of men's wear is designed, stitched, and packaged by a team of designers and other business professionals. It's no mystery how the Trumps and Oprah's of the world keep getting richer and richer. Many endorsements such as Andre Agassi's Nike campaign earned him millions more than he would have ever made just playing tennis.

Even though most people will never get a chance to endorse a product, **anyone with an idea and some ingenuity and tenacity can break into the royalties market through licensing their idea/product or getting a celebrity to endorse for it.** Royalty rates can range from as low as 3% up to 20% or more. Rates and advances against projected sales should always be negotiable.

Don't waste another moment. Think of something you can do to claim your share of this booming yet obscure opportunity.

Things to License:

Information (newsletters, videos, workshops, tapes, etc)
Clothes
Characters
Slogans
Greeting Cards/Art

Tip: Marekting for Dummies says the best way to keep your product in the public eye is to constantly reinvent the packaging and keep campaigns updated. This way you can compete with other or newer and exciting products. As the rightful owner of a product one can also maintain subsidiary rights to create spin off products later down the road.

#10 The Money Merge Account

Definition: The MMA (money merge account) incorporates your checking and savings with an advanced line of credit or HELOC. Through this program, homeowners have the ability to pay off their 30 year mortgage in as little as one-third of the time, without refinancing their existing mortgage loan or increasing minimum monthly payments because you will be using the HELOC to help pay down the debt rather than use it on frivolous things. MMA is the fastest way to repay a mortgage.

Your 30 year mortgage can now be paid off in 8-11 years. Compare the charts below to see what you will save with the MMA account using the same calculations.

MMA Program

$136,058 mortgage
$126,032 in 1 year
11.33 years repayment time
$45,159 total interest paid

Conventional

$136,058 mortgage
$126,032 in 4.7 years
30 years to repay
$134,726 interest paid

A 30 yr, $136,000 mortgage at 5.25%, when paid through conventional monthly payments, will result in a 30 year total repayment of $270,784—nearly twice the cost of the home. The MMA program can repay the same mortgage in 11.3 yrs with a total repayment of $181,217. A savings of $89,217 is realized on the same income, with the same mortgage, at the same interest rate, and without any changes to your standard of living.

Tip: When refinancing double check fees. If you are paying points, make sure you get the best rate for those points.—C. McCorery, Realtor

Tip Two: Bi-Weekly mortgage payments will reduce a 30 year mortgage to 23 years, allowing to pay off your debt and make more equity available sooner.

#11 Cha Ching: Vending

Ahhh, the sound of "Cha-Ching" always puts a smile on just about everybody's face. If you like the sound of money cascading out of a slot machine at the casinos, imagine hearing "cha-ching' once or twice per week from your own vending machines.

Vending is a special all cash business. You can make a fortune on other people's small change.

This is the perfect business for "the gambler" type of business person. The" gambler entrepreneur" invests strictly for quick cash flow. He or she deals very little with customers because the product sells itself, night and day, 24/7.

Entrepreneurs who love to build relationships and are good at marketing and attracting clients I refer to as "the negotiators." They are also highly persuasive and tend to operate service businesses like homecare for the elderly or nutritional consultation.

Here is a list of Cha-Ching Ventures

-
Coin Laundry
Soda Pop/Snack Machines
Slot Machines
Bingo/Raffle
Hot Dog/Coffee Cart Vending
Coin Operated Massage Chairs

#12 Dividend Reinvestment Plan

One of the most important messages I want this book to instill in the poorer population of America is to learn to do more than just work, save, and borrow money. Learn to make money hustle for you for a change. Invest your money now.

A good way to start is to open a DRIP or Dividend Reinvestment Plan. These investment plans minimize risks, cut cost because you handle them yourself, and they have many advantages over mutual funds.

Many financial experts have said mutual funds usually consist of questionable fees, poor performance, and that most investors do not know which companies are owned by the fund.

Over a trillion dollars of 401k money is locked in poor performing mutual funds.

DRIPs are offered by companies to encourage the small investor to own shares in various companies directly, bypassing brokerage commissions that can be more costly than the cost of shares themselves.

Dividend reinvestment plans allow the shareholder to strategize in two ways:

1. Dollar-Cost Averaging
2. Diversify Assets

Dollar-Cost Averaging lets the investor invest with a fixed sum of dollars on a regular basis. This helps you buy more shares when prices are low and less when shares are high. **DRIP investing is based on dollar amount purchases rather than share amount purchases, allowing whole or fractional shares to be acquired.**

Diversification allows investors to start small in a large number of companies and build their portfolios slowly and methodically over time. If you go through a broker like Charles Schwab, you will initially buy in lots of 100 shares which can cost $1,000-$5,000. Most people find $1,000 or more too risky and will end up not investing at all.

Remember stocks are segregated into **growth and value** groupings. Growth tends to pay little in dividends and value stock pays more in dividends. It's important to note that older companies are more reliable and happy to pay out dividends. However, they are not obligated to distribute any at all if this is the decision of the board.

Spread your risks out by investing in several Drips. When one plan is down, but another is stable or up, you won't feel compelled to sell the low performing stock. Hold on for the long term, not the short term to get the full benefit of compounding stock offers.

Go to Directinvesting. Com for more information. The website is very informative and gets you started immediately.

They also publish The Money Paper's Direct Investing Newsletter twice per month providing detailed portfolios of DRIP companies, investing recommendations, focused strategies to get better results, online access to investment content, and professional advice and guidance from Executive Editor Dave Fish.

Tips: Reits, Food, Health, and Technology are some of the fastest growing DRIPs. Make sure to invest in one of these industries.

#13 Buying a Business v. Starting One

Do you have a unique vision for a new business venture? Do you think it will change the world as we know it like Microsoft or Google? Does the venture enable you to dominate a niche no one has discovered? Last but not least, do you possess the financials to get it up and running for the first three years? If you answered yes to nearly all the questions, then maybe you should start a business from the ground up.

Starting your own business is not the only way to get into business. You can buy one and save yourself money, time, and energy. Self-employment is the American dream come true. It means freedom and control over what you do. When you buy a business, everything is ready to go. You will have a customer base and a good idea about the financial projections. Sometimes the seller will train and get you up to speed on how to handle customer relations and procedures.

The amount required as a down payment when purchasing an established business runs 10% to 20%. A $50,000 down payment will help purchase a business valued at $250,000.

Service oriented businesses can be operated by one person or a large group of people. In the past most of these businesses were set up in a commercial space, but more and more entrepreneurs are working from home.

There are sweet advantages to going it alone from home. Here are a few high-lights a go-it-alone business offers:

1. You're the Boss

2. No employees

3. Little or no overhead

4. Flex Time

5. You can concentrate on core activities and outsource services you cannot handle due to time constraints or lack of expertise.

If you like excitement and rather have a fast paced, high profile business, consider the domain of mass communications or media.

Most people are under the impression this area is reserved only for actors, filmmakers, magazine, and broadcast professionals. With the emergence of Myspace.com and Youtube.com, and online radio stations, the younger generation is breaking down the walls that prevented the average person from showcasing their talents to the world.

Anyone interested in the media can start a small media empire. For example, a newsletter or website or video blog has the potential to flourish into a major online or printed magazine or television show. Some bloggers have been offered book deals as well.

You can produce a reality, talk, or variety show at your local public access station. Then present it to network executives to see if they will pick it up. *Use an entertainment attorney to expedite the process.*

Oprah started in radio. American Radio Network (ARN) in Los Angeles, California offers free radio training to its members who produce shows for the network of stations owned by ARN. Producers learn to find sponsors to support and pay for shows. ARN also provides members with a press pass which must be surrendered upon resignation. Radio production is definitely less stressful. I produced two shows by myself at ARN and sometimes invited my sister to act as a co-host.

EBooks and CD's can be produced on a personal computer and your home video series can be edited and packaged at a professional facility. This is where you should consider self-publishing or zero cost media joint ventures/licensing to get the video or cd distributed.

Media training requires a very small investment. Enroll in any free training programs you can find and keep in touch with classmates because radio and TV shows are difficult to produce solo. Also, buy some of your own equipment. As a producer, you will wear many hats.

Producers scout for talent, locations, arrange for catering and studio time. They also raise the funds, oversee the budget, schedule the shoot, and supervise production assistants and so on. These tasks can be assigned to crew members if you can afford them.

Tip: Keep business expenses down and buy the building where you conduct business—D. Bach

Tip Two: Make sure your business has potential for expansion. Look for opportunities that will create residual income. For instance, a spa business can offer spa products, retreats, spa parties, workshops, etc. It can go beyond simple massage and body wrap services. Residual income will free up your time, keep money flowing into the business without you having to be present all the time, thus preventing you from becoming a "wage slave" to your own business.

#14 Courtesy Deposits

Courtesy Deposits can be applied to the following situations:

- Business loans
- line of credits
- real estate developers
- investors
- residential mortgages
- business ownership
- business start ups
- business acquisitions
- franchise purchases
- bridge loans
- equipment
- working capital
- capitalization needs
- venture capital
- retail stores

A Courtesy Deposit (a.k.a. Deposit Capital) enhances your capital seeking campaign by providing incentive for the lender to fund your package. These deposits are attached to your loan package, line of credit request, or business project in order to make your proposal for capital more appealing to your lender. Courtesy Deposits can also provide the lender with liquidity for your loan and other loans.

Deposit Capital comes with certain strict requirements and large fees. The rules are they can never be encumbered, pledged, put in jeopardy, used to collateralize your loan, or used to guarantee your loan. Your lender does not have the right of offset against deposits. No funds can or will be deposited into your bank account. Only your banker will have access to the funds used to purchase Jumbo CD's ($100K and up) at the bank.

Courtesy Deposits are an excellent resource for established companies or start ups with an initial large sum of working capital.

#15 Low Start Ups

"Those who have failed to work towards the truth have missed the purpose of living"

—*Buddha*

There are hundreds of business specializations you can choose from today if your goal is to become financially independent. Make sure to choose a specialization that you absolutely love. I cannot emphasize this enough. I tried to start a Day Care with a friend which I'll talk more about in a later chapter. It did not work because I was not in love with it. The city in which we lived had a large demand for child care and my friend had several years of experience in this area, and I had the house and money, so it seemed like a good thing to pursue.

Don't do what we did. Go for something that springs from a hobby or talent which could ultimately lead to a unique niche no one else is doing. Make sure your heart is in it.

Low start up businesses usually require $5,000 or less. Set aside money from your budget to cover the following items:

Business cards
Stationary
Fax Machine
Office Supplies
Petty Cash for Mileage, etc.

Vistaprint.com charges reasonable rates for business cards, postcards, etc. Check them out.

Also take the time to design several publicity materials before you open your business in order to avoid fumbling for them when potential clients ask you for information.

Publicity Materials include but are not limited to:

Brochures
Press Release
Bio
Photos of yourself
Advertising Specialties (pens, mugs, post-its)

The rest of your funds should handle the bulk of inventory needed for operations. A resale permit will help you (the vendor) purchase merchandise at wholesale prices and then sell at retail to turn a profit.

LIST OF LOW START UP BUSINESSES

Gift Baskets	Wine Club
Online Magazine	Wedding/Event Planning
Massage Therapy	Art Classes
Candle Making	Soap Making
Greeting Cards	Book Writing
Editing Service	Consultation
Publicity/PR	Floral Arranging
Speaking/Hosting	Personal Assistant
Personal Chef	Stylist
Life Coach	Private Investigation

34

LIST OF LOW START UP BUSINESSES (Continued)

Website Developer	Interior Decorating
Landscape Design	Photography
Retreat Specialist	Spa Party Planner
Make Up Artist	Exercise Trainer
Dating Service	Resume Writer
Yoga Instructor	Tour Guide
Small Day Care	House Sitting
Pet Sitting	Agent
Product Development	Internet Retail Store
Online Gallery	Pottery/Sculpture
Nanny Service	Comic Strip Artist
Handbags/Jewelry Line	Motivational Workshop

#16 Rich Kid/Poor Kid ...

Which one will your child be?

You can help shape your child's financial destiny.

Learn how with The Seeds of Wealth, a wealth building program that can jump start a financially free life style for your children now ... you can even save a million dollars for yourself, too.

If you have children between the ages of 1 through 21, I urge you to take a few minutes to deeply reflect on the future of their finances.

There is absolutely no excuse for any child today to face a life of financial struggle or a destitute retirement anymore.

Research reports that approximately $1,520 is passed down from parents, relatives, family friends, and odd jobs to children each year which can be invested in their future.

It has been proven by many sources on how to attract abundance (such as *The Seeds of Wealth Savings, Investment, and Financial Education Program*) that poverty is the direct result of never learning sound savings and investment strategies as children.

The majority of older Americans who are experiencing impoverishment issues unfortunately inherited their parent's inability to create wealth, and, they learned the same crippling behavior from their parents ... a vicious cycle that still continues to plague thousands of people today.

But there is hope. This vicious cycle can be stopped in its track simply by implementing several coveted secrets on how to build wealth for your child as well as yourself even if you do not have an above average income. In fact, in a few moments we will look at a special savings method your children can start practicing today.

If you want your kids to have no major financial worries, then *Seeds of Wealth* is a good option. Packed with 308 pages of invaluable savings, investment, and educational tools that will not only build security but instill in your children the ability to think BIG about money.

Even prominent CEO's, Real Estate Guru's, and motivational speakers claim their number one secret to success is "thinking big."

When kids think big early in life, they develop a positive relationship with money. In turn it's easier to make money work for you rather than you for it.

Watch as your children's money grow from a mere $2 a day investment into $25,000 by age 13, $60,000 by age 18, $123,000 by 23 and so ... all the way to $9-10 Million by age 55.

The *Seeds of Wealth* program makes it possible for your children to retire when they are still relatively young, vital, and productive so they can pursue other interests if they want to.

Nothing is more desirable than having freedom to choose what one wants to do and be able to do it ... which comes easy when money is not an issue.

TIP: The tale of two card board boxes

Remember the $1,520 I mentioned earlier? Well, half of it can be easily saved by using two cardboard boxes. One will be used for spending ... the other for saving. When you divide $1,520 by 2 you get $760 per year which breaks down to $2 per day.

That's all your child needs to stash away to get started on the road to riches.

Not only is this a fun way to save money, but once you get started, it will develop into a habit and you won't be able to stop ... nor will you want too once you begin to see this money blossom day by day via guidance from *Seeds of Wealth*.

Contact: Seeds of Wealth, 808 St. Paul Street, Baltimore, MD 21202 or just Google Seeds of Wealth online.

#17 Other Types of Real Estate

As you probably know already, real estate is the foundation of some of the fortunes of the riches people in the world. There is a huge amount of information on the market today that will teach you how to build a real estate portfolio. Look for books in the real estate section of your bookstore on flipping, foreclosures, tax lien certificates, and REO's (banked own properties). My favorite authors to look for are Tyler Hicks and Robert Kiyosaki.

Because real estate is flexible, a person can choose to invest or work as a real estate professional in financing, property management, sales, appraisal, and development.

The main objective in building a real estate empire is to leverage property that will produce a monthly cash flow using OPM—other people's money. Serious investors buy, fix, and sell up to four to six single family properties or two or three multi-unit properties per year and manage their tenants themselves or hire a property management company to oversee leasing and maintenance. Once investors reach at least one million in assets they start buying commercial buildings which range from offices to warehouses. Most hard money lenders offer up to 70 LTV when lending money for commercial real estate.

Converting old apartments into high end condos is now a popular way to create large profits. For example, if you purchase a ten unit building for $800K and sell each unit for $300K (10 x 300K=$3,000,000) which can easily pay back all loans and produce a cushy profit. When converting apartments into condos you must obtain a separate deed for each unit before putting the condo up for sale.

Real estate is a competitive business. The best time to get in is during a "in between" or buyer's market. Too much overbidding occurs during a seller's market and you may end up paying more than what the property is worth, so be careful. Just two properties alone can increase an average person's net worth to a million or more instantly.

There are many other types of real estate to consider purchasing other than residential and office buildings. They include:

1.   Parking Lots

2.   Trailers/Campers

3.   Boats/Yachts

4.   Marinas

5.   Golf Courses

6.   Hotels/Mixed Used

TIP: Get a personal loan to cover down or get seller to carry a second for you. Then refinance in 6–12 months to pay seller back.

#18 Use Lease Options to Create Cash Flow

Back in March, I attended The Learning Annex Wealth and Real Estate Expo. One of the mini workshops I attended with my sister, Carmen, talked about Leasing with the Option to Buy. This is a great way to create cash flow if you own your home or several homes and feel it's time to unload them.

Lease Options provide individuals and couples a way to buy property they otherwise would have a difficult time getting. **A lease option is an agreement between a buyer and a seller that allows the buyer to lock in the future purchase price, save money for a down payment and buy the property in the future at current prices.**

The lease with option to buy can be arranged for a 1-2 year period. There are two components to consider with a lease with option to buy:

1. Option Money
2. Rent

The purchase money is a large sum of cash paid to the seller, usually somewhere between $5,000 to $10,000, upfront. This fee will be deducted from the price of the property when the time comes and is regarded as part of the down payment.

Rent money can be raised as high as the market rents will bear.

And option money is a small sum of money that goes on top of the rent. If the lessee/tenant fails to purchase the property, the purchase money and option money will be forfeited.

When an investor uses this strategy he/she approaches a troubled home owner with the option to buy and usually secures his/her position by offering to pay for payments in arrears (which is recouped over the term of the lease option) and finds the new tenant. It is often considered undesirable by investors to spend any money, but if it cannot be avoided, start with $500.

The lease-option form can be located at a real estate company or at the Board of Realtors Association.

How it Works

1. Agree with the seller on a purchase price

2. Agree on the term of lease (1-2 years)

3. Determine a market value for your monthly rent. Add $25-500 on to top of rent called option money. It is not required, but it is what creates the cash flow and accumulates money for a down payment.

4. Agree upon terms regarding the exercise of the option's escrow period and financing. Have a real estate attorney look over the papers.

5. Determine who pays for the inspections, work and warranties when it comes to complete the purchase.

6. Handle the transaction as a lease until you are ready to exercise the option. Make sure it's in writing.

7. Open escrow or contact a real estate attorney to handle the transaction.

Other Things to Think About

Escrow is not needed until you exercise your option to buy

If you do not exercise the option to buy, all option money and additional rent monies paid to the seller are nonrefundable.

All terms of the purchase must be clear and agreed upon at the time you create the lease-option agreement.

You will have to decide to either forfeit your option money or pay the originally agreed upon price if the price of the house goes down.

The papers will go to the lender to show proof of down payment made over the course of the agreed upon term.

#19 Inc Yourself

There are several benefits to inc-ing yourself. Incorporating protects assets and allows a business to raise capital through stock.

When you first decide to raise capital by issuing stock, the first round is referred to as the owners or founder's shares. Founders should buy 60% to make sure they maintain ownership position for at least one year. As the companies initial board of directors, they can set the value at whatever price they decide on.

The second round is usually opened to friends, family, and other professional confidants such as a lawyer or accountant. This is when the value is raised slightly higher. Six months later, outside investors are invited to buy shares. This is the PPO or Private Placement Offering.

In California corporations are exempt from franchise tax the first year. Nevada is the best state to incorporate if you want to avoid the high cost of doing business in California.

WHY NEVADA?

1. No state or corporate tax

2. Directors, Officers, and shareholders do not have to hold meetings in Nevada

3. Flexible arrangements for debt and equity holdings

4. No information sharing agreement with the IRS

5.   Low Filing fees for Officer's List and Registered Agency

The IPO (Invest Public Offering) can take place to raise several million before any business operation starts or after an established private company wishes "to go public."

Nolo Press Books and *Incorporating for Dummies* are excellent sources on how to incorporate. You can also consult a lawyer and obtain inexpensive incorporation services at www.inc-it-now.com.

#20 Buy Ugly ... Sell Ugly

Do you want to flip a property, but you're not handy?

Well, there's good news for you. Flipping no longer has to involve complete renovation of a property.

Savvy investors can now turn a profit without getting their hands dirty. Not all investors enjoy fixing up run downs nor do they have the time.

Instead of buying ugly and selling pretty they do the exact opposite: Buy ugly and sell ugly with a slightly marked up priced. The latest buyers market of 2006-2007 has also made flipping short sales possible that are usually banked own and in better condition than fixers.

Take a look at how a short sale can put cash in your fist today:

- Price investor sells the house for = $400,000
- Price paid for the house by the investor= $375,000
- Difference=Gross Profit= $25,000
- Closing costs, and miscellaneous expenses= $ 5,000
- Net Profit for the investor=$20,000

The flipping process can be a fast or slow and the quality of work depends on the help you hire. You may find your original budget stretched to the limit due to unexpected repairs. Make sure to integrate a 10% contingency into the budget for emergencies.

URB, a rehab company in Chicago, reminds us not to get greedy. Start with small properties that can yield $25-$35,000 in profit.

Buy several run downs and package them "as is" to another investor who actually likes to gut a property and remodel it.

Tip: To locate hot property areas hang out at night to see what's going on at night. Other good indicators are schools, influx of jobs, young people, and Starbucks.

—Barbara Corcoran

#21 The Law of Attraction

There are several good books available on The Law of Attraction. One is entitled *The Secret* and the other is *The Law of Attraction* by Michael Losier.

You must read one of these books if you want to help change your life.

I think it's important to talk a little about this phenomenon. Knowing how to work with the law of attraction will help you examine your belief system and make the necessary changes to bring you the things you want.

Until you know how to work in this manner you will, like I have in the past as well as many other people, attract the opposite of what you want or attract the undesirable unless you are a very, very lucky person.

Life Coach and motivational speaker, Iyanla Van Zant, said it perfectly on the television show, *Starting Over*. She said, "You attract not what you want but what you believe."

What you want and what you believe are two different things and can cause inner spiritual conflict. The early part of my life seemed to attract the bizarre or undesirable situation because of this very reason. I sent out too many conflicting messages to the universe, so it did not know what to give me.

The first thing I did to prevent this from happening was to call back all the pieces of myself. My energy was scattered and I had to learn to center myself. Meditation became the tool I used to calm my mind, stay focused, and mindful. I spent an entire year isolating myself to meditate and realign myself with my life's purpose. It was the best year of my life.

Shortly after that year ended I started reading Anthony Robbin's *Unlimited Power*, *Awaken the Giant Within*, and listened to his *Live With Passion* seminar on Cd.

I began working with the tools he outlines in his book. I definitely cannot explain it better than him, so go out and buy the books. Here are some tools for working with the Law of Attraction:

1. Get clear. This suggest you must be clear about what you want and do not want in your life

2. Prepare a statement on what you want to attract into your life. There's nothing more powerful than writing. The second thing you must do is write down what you want in your life.

3. Finally, *allow* the universe to help you attract your desires. In other words, do not fret or obsess on whether or not you'll get what you want and when it will arrive. Just trust the universe. Wish upon a star and let the universe do the rest.

The Law of Attraction is a tool to help you realize your dreams and be successful. It deals with positive energy only. Negative energy blocks what you want.

Try it. You have nothing to lose and everything to gain.

#22 Your Relationship With Money Checklist

Circle Yes or No to each question below.

1. Is money always lacking in your life? Yes/No

2. Do you find value in pennies? Yes/No

3. Are you living below the median income level? Yes/No

4. Do you give money on a monthly basis or a 10% tithe to a nonprofit organization or church? Yes/No

5. Do you expect your significant other to give you money? Yes/No

6. Do you sometimes give money to friends, family or acquaintances without expecting it back? Yes/No

7. Is society to blame for the financial rut your in, if you're in one? Yes/No.

8. Do you spend more than you save? Yes/No

9. Is your credit 680 and up? Yes/No

10. Do you love money? Yes/No

MY INSIGHT ON THE ABOVE ANSWERS

1. If money is always lacking because of salary or bills try to increase your salary or cut down the bills. Usually people live beyond their means so even if you increase your salary research shows that most

people continue to spend all their money and feel they are still in the same rut. Isolate the increase and save it.

2. If you find value in a penny your relationship with money is an honorable one. Suze Orman once told a woman that her $700 in savings was a lot of money, but the woman didn't see it the same way. The lesson of the story is "every penny counts."

3. If you're living below the median income level it's time to demand more of yourself. Find a way to supplement your income. Start a business or look into new vocational training in a field with higher pay.

4. Just giving some of your money to a cause you care about puts good energy in the air. It will come back to you. It usually does when we least expect it and sometimes it is not always monetary, but you'll recognize it when it does appear.

5. I hope you always say thank you when your significant other gives you money. Remember money does not grow on trees. He or she worked hard or smart for it and it should be seen as a gift from the Gods down to you.

6. If you can really spare it, then it's okay to help someone out once in a while. No doubt they will feel special and view you as a special friend.

7. We are all guilty of blaming our problems on something. Many of our problems can be traced back to the dishonesty or interference from others, but sooner or later we are left alone to deal with the issue. No one can fix it but you. Get a pen, pad, and start brainstorming solutions. Take action. Take control over all your problems.

8. Time to curb this bad habit. Saving some of your earnings teaches discipline and it's the only way to make it grow.

9. If your credit is 680 or higher—congrats! This is a good indicator that you are a good money manager. Shoot for 680 and up to get credit increases and good rates on home loans as well as the respect of your family.

10. Love money in a healthy sense. Don't steal or kill for it. Just appreciate the ways it can enhance your life.

#23 Upping Your Standards

When I made it my mission to study successful people I saw they had one thing in common: higher standards.

They expected better results in everything which included demands they placed on others and themselves.

They had little tolerance for the ordinary.

Upping your standards=change.

I want you to up your standards in regards to something that is outdated and moldy in your life right now.

Tell yourself you want better and expect a difference today. This is all you have to do. It's a matter of getting rid of the old so the new can enter like a breath of fresh air.

#24 Choose A High Paying Vocation

Not everyone believes four years of college is the ideal path to follow.

Make sure to choose a high paying vocation, if you do not pursue college because you have to earn a living.

Do not take just any job. There are too many mediocre jobs that will never pay more than minimum wage or $10 per hour.

Look for a field that you love and that is closely related to a favorite hobby.

Your employer should offer benefits, the salary you want, and cost of living increases.

Remember to pay yourself first. Put 10% of your earnings each month into an orange or E*trade savings account.

The following is a list of high paying vocations with pay. A student out of high school can start training for one of these vocations immediately and earn an above average pay.

1. Chef $80k-100K after 3-5 years

2. Pharmacy Tech $18-20 Hr

3. Medical Assistant $35K up

4. Nurse $80K year

5. Court Reporter $65-110K year

6. Sales, unlimited earnings. Look for base pay plus commission. Sales can be in real estate, cars, etc.

7. Casino Dealer $3,000 month or more

8. Massage/Physical Therapy $35K up

9. Paralegal $40K up

10. Auto Tech $35K up

11. Personal Assistant $50K-$100K

12. Financial Advisor $50K to $100k

13. Copywriting $50k to $100K

Better than a high paying vocation is buying or starting your own business.

This way you do not end up afraid to take risks and being a "wage slave."

Tip: Visit www.calapprenticeships.org

#25 The Five Enemies

What are the five enemies?

The Buddhist teach there are five enemies (also called the five hindrances) that are the root cause of unhappiness in human beings.

Whenever we are determined to go after our dreams, we will be faced with an up hill battle. If we want to win the war, our mind must be strong, clear, and focused.

There will be desert periods … obstacles … frustration … distractions … sometimes things will work out just fine and sometimes things will fall apart. One minute there's happiness and progress; then next there's anger and sadness which can lead some people to behave in a selfish manner.

This is why everyone should be aware of these five negative emotional states which can always be transformed into positive emotional states.

The five enemies are:

- Anger
- Restlessness and Worry
- Doubt
- Sloth of the Mind
- Sensual or Selfish Desire

You can refer to my book, *The Five Enemies*, also published by Iuniverse to learn more.

The best way to handle these emotions when they rise up in you is to: 1) Recognize the emotion. Stare it right between the eyes: 2) Do not let it feed off of you in any way. Have an "interrupt" ready. An "interrupt" is something you say inside your head that immediately ushers in a happy thought. Use it to replace or transform the negative emotion, and: 3) Practice, practice, practice. One day this will become a very natural thing to do.

#26 Narrow Your Options

Too many interests = too many options.

Too many options= burn out and confusion.

I remember being very focused during childhood. Most people are. When we are young and free there is clarity. That clarity unfortunately disappeared by the time I graduated from high school and enrolled in college. A whole new world of different careers opened up to me, careers I never knew existed.

I remember having to weigh one against the other and suddenly could not make up my mind. I eventually chose to major in the cinematic arts.

The main reason things went haywire in my life had to with the pressure to work as well as the type of work I took on to earn a living while in school.

If you are in a position of not having to work while studying for a degree, I advise to remain steadfast in your position until you graduate because part time jobs can burn you out and take priority sometimes over studies.

My workload on top of homework drove me up the wall. I worked in offices and retail stores—neither which I liked. I ended up job hopping and burning myself out to the point where school suddenly took a back seat and filmmaking was dealt with on the side. My dream of being a filmmaker never blossomed in the way I had hoped for.

Narrow your options in order to stay focused. Consider no more than two ventures at a time. Most likely you will get somewhere in a shorter amount of time without running out of steam and going a little nuts.

#27 Never Stop Learning

It's an old worn out cliché, but it still has merit! You should never stop learning.

I love reading, writing, and discovering how and why people do the things they do.

Learning is a life long process. The planet is our classroom.

The more you know … the better off you will be intellectually, emotionally, and spiritually.

Try to read a good book at least three times a year, take a workshop at the local community college or adult center, and teach yourself a new skill like painting, typing, or bowling.

Expand…. grow…. be resourceful!

For those who do not like to read, listen to books on cd. Listen to them as many times as you can whether in your car or at your desk.

#28 Your Credit: How To Use it Wisely

First of all in order to have great credit you have to have some credit.

Having no credit is worst than having bad credit.

Credit scores range from 300-850. The median score is around 723. You need high scores to get the best rates.

Home lenders will base pre-approval for a 100%, stated loan on mid scores 680 up, so keep it high.

You can receive a free credit report once per year from **Annual Credit Report.Com.**, set up by federal law. The free credit report you see advertised on commercials are not free. There is a usually a charge for credit monitoring or a fee disguised as a processing fee. Annual Credit Report.Com is a consumer agency and you are entitled to one free report every year.

If you have no credit or need to repair credit apply for a merchant card. Fingerhut has helped many people restore their credit worthiness.

To keep your credit under control, do not use more than 50% of your total credit. For example, if you have 5 credit cards and the credit lines total $6,000 do not use more than $3,000. If you use more, creditors will think you do not have control over credit.

I have no merchant cards at the moment because I have disciplined myself not to shop frivolously for clothes, accessories, and what I call "Junk" items. I do not let the media and other people pressure me into buying unnecessary products. Merchant cards encourage shopping, so when you open a Fingerhut account I advise keeping the balance down to no more than $25.00 rather than closing it.

Closing accounts as well as applying for too many cards can bring down your score. Every time an inquiry is made, your credit score decreases.

Always pay your cards 5 to 7 days before the due date. Late payments are hard to remove off credit reports. They remain on the report for up to a year and bring down your score by 40-50 points.

The wisest ways to use your credit is on real estate, starting a business or buying a business, and on common stock.

Some individuals have $50,000, $75,000 or more in credit. This borrowed money can jump start you on the road to riches. You will need money to make money and have to sacrifice your savings or borrowed money again and again in order to build wealth.

100,000 new millionaires emerge each year and some have used credit to get there.

Call your creditors to **increase your credit** every year and try to **eliminate any annual fees** and **decrease your rates** if you can. Credit increases make your score go up believe it or not.

Again, try not to buy petty things with credit. Use credit to increase your net worth. This is what high net worth people do.

Tip: Advice above from the "school of hard knocks."

#29 The "Pre" in Tax Dollars and Ipo's

Want to get your hands on your money before the IRS does and get in on shares before they go public and go up in price?

Then open and start feeding your 401k with pre-tax dollars. Hopefully your employer will also match 25, 50, or 100% to make your retirement grow faster.

The Pre IPO is no stranger to corporate business men and women, but it is to the rest of us.

The average citizen who has little financial literacy is usually clueless about IPO's, let alone Pre IPO's. Consult with a good financial adviser who can explain what it is in more detail and how you can participate in one.

IPO's, Initial Public Offering, is when a corporation goes public, allowing the public to buy shares. The key to making an IPO work for you is before it goes public. You want to be in like Flynn during the Pre-IPO stage.

Pre-IPO investing involves buying a stake in a company before its initial public offering of securities. The shares may be as low as 10 cents. You can buy an incredible amount of shares at this price. When the IPO goes public, the shares are offered at higher prices to triple your ROI.

Pre IPO's that go public have made shareholders rich over night.

Again, consult with a financial advisor to find out more about them if you do not have a relative or friend who owns a business and is planning to go public. If you have a friend or relative who is about to launch an IPO, give them all the money you can spare.

There are risks whenever you invest. Pre IPO's promise big returns. Beware of pre IPOS offered through emails or e-commerce. Often they are fraudulent.

Internet Pre IPO's, according to a report by at http://www.sec.gov/investor/pubs/preipo.htm may be:1. Illegal: 2. Unregistered. Pre IPO's should be registered with the SEC, U.S. Securities and Exchange Commission or prove exemption and: 3. the company may never go public which means you will not recover your investment.

Exempt companies are not allowed to advertise the offering or make solicitations to the public. It is held in secrecy.

Always conduct research on the following point:

1. Get full details about the offering

2. Get information on the company

3. Get information on management

4. Find out the identity of the underwriter who may or may not exist.

5. Get the identity and disciplinary history of the promoter.

Be skeptical about internet offerings and see a good financial advisor, attorney or your state securities regulator. You can also see **SEC's Public Reference Room** to check if a company has filed an offering circular under Reg A or a Form D under Regulation D.

#30 Keep A Personal Balance Sheet

A balance sheet documents your financial position and should be updated every month.

You can track your expenses and see if you are accomplishing your goals.

You will know where all your money went at the end of the month.

They are simple to prepare. Most balance sheets are one page in length.

See the example format below.

Your Name
Month and year

Assets (what you own/income)	Liabilities (debts)
Cash on Hand $	Credit Cards$
Furniture	Loans
Equipment	Home Loan
New Home	Auto
Total $	Total $

Assets-Liabilities = Net Worth

Tip: You will want to keep your net worth in the positive. If it's negative, work on reducing some of your debt.

#31 Is Money Really The Root Of All Evil?

This question has posed an interesting argument for many centuries. The belief that money is the root of all evil has been engrained in all of us.

Lack of money has caused many headaches … major financial crises … hunger … even horrific scandals between family members, lovers, and friends across the globe.

It's our frustration with money that perpetuates the belief it is evil.

If this is your view, I want you to crush that thought. Completely get rid of it. It's time for a new attitude.

Start thinking of money as your friend, a friend that will help you and support you in your time of need.

When I let go of this old way of thinking about money and looked at it as my non judgmental friend, I started to do more to make more. I buckled down and wrote books, exercised more, ate healthier, meditated, and enjoyed my life more.

Most important my new relationship with money lead to raises in pay. My friends gave me money for my birthday and creditors increased my credit. You name it—things were looking up!

Appreciate and celebrate the money that flows into your life and it will return the favor.

#32 The Free Agent Man (or Woman)

Are you a bit nervous about leaving your job to enter the realm of entrepreneurship?

Unfortunately, a lot of people dream about going-it-alone as their own boss, but are afraid. We are all born entrepreneurs, but our culture grooms us to be worker bees first, sometimes stomping out completely our innate abilities to make unlimited income through entrepreneurial pursuits.

I want you to get your "mojo" back.

A good way to make the transition from employee to entrepreneur is to work as a part time free agent for a short period of time. Do this on the side and try to double or triple your earnings.

A free agent or independent contractor has control over several things.

The free agent chooses his/her assignments and determines his/her pay.

As a free agent, you will responsible for paying your own taxes. When responding to an assignment, offer a brochure of services in lieu of a resume. This will automatically place you in a power position as a force to be reckoned with. It's important to maintain this dynamic to be treated like an expert.

I recommend going this route to get a taste of what it might be like to be free without giving up your day job right away. Eventually you will come to the point where you will quit your day job and work as a full time free agent.

A full time free agent can remain a sole proprietor or set up his or her business as a LLC or Corporation.

#33 Balancing the Spiritual While Pursuing the Material

Because this world has a negative energy field and we are born of the flesh, our needs tend to focus on the material rather than spiritual matters for self-preservation. Life is about getting as much as we can. Some of us stock up on more than our share, referred to as "greed.'

Rarely do we think about slowing down in the fast paced society to take a deep breath and get in touch with our souls. I struggled with trying to balance my spirituality with the pursuit of materialism for many years. Then I came across the book, *Being In Balance*, by Dr. Wayne Dyer. He believes a person can restore complete balance by focusing on work 50% of the time and focusing on spirituality 50% of the time.

Edgar Cayce also noticed this imbalance and recommended 8 hours rest, 8 hours play, and 8 hours work which equaled a perfectly balanced 24 hour day. We, however, tend to work 10-15 hours, and the rest of the hours are spent cramming shopping, cooking, and sleeping into whatever is left. This is perhaps the reason why so many people suffer from insomnia and anxiety.

Try to get in touch with your spirit once per week … or even better, do a little soul searching every day. Take a few minutes to pray for your health, family and friends, and the welfare of the planet when you wake up in the morning.

Find a quiet place where you can concentrate and rid yourself of all the self talk or chatter in your mind. Listen to the trees rustle, the birds sing, and the rain tap against your window.

Go within and listen for messages from the depth of your soul.

Feed the soul regularly by raising your vibrational energy and by practicing good deeds. Take the road less traveled rather than the safe and familiar one all the time. This will help you reach a higher level of enlightenment.

Learn from mistakes. Try to do something better than you've done before. Avoid pattern behavior and repeating mistakes.

One of the best ways to get out from under an ordeal that you are very attached to is to forgive the situation and let go. Don't obsess. Just visualize a lot of positive white light around your body and the situation and it will begin to heal.

Your spiritual wealth will enrich your life in ways cold hard cash will never be able to.

SECTION TWO
Business Tool Box Workbook

This workbook is broken down into several exercises on mind-set, how to get started on designing a product, and what do include in a business plan.

Your Mind Set

"Stubbornness reacts. Determination initiates."

—Linda Goodman, Astrologer

According to creative visualization leader, Shakti Gawain, and many other psychologists, our negative core beliefs are formed during the early stages of our lives. They are deep seated and often contribute to undesirable experiences in our lives.

An example of a negative thought looks like this: I don't trust myself. I don't know if I can handle being the boss."

This kind of thinking immediately sets you up to experience negative trust issues. Being in opposition with yourself will attract those who will be against you as well.

Another example may be: "I'll probably just break even and never increase my profit." This belief can only bring you one thing—difficulty in making a profit. To overcome lack of confidence put yourself in a state of certainty. Know you will be victorious.

Spiritual leader, Dr. Wayne Dyer, has emphasized in several of his books the universe will deliver what you believe. **If you believe something will not work, then it will not; if you believe something will work, then it will.**

List two negative core beliefs you may have about starting a business and rewrite them in the form of a positive belief. This is the cure. Replace all negative thoughts with positive thoughts for 30 days, the time it takes to fully change a mental habit permanently.

Core Belief # 1

_____

Replace With:

_____

Core Belief #2

_____

Replace With:

_____

Remember, do this exercise for 30 days and keep a journal that will document the changes in your attitude.

Overcoming Your Fear

We all fear doing certain things from time to time. Fear can stop us in our tracks and prevent us from doing the things we really want to do.

Minister, Joyce Meyers, defines fear as **"false evidence appearing real."** What she means by this is we tend to create negative scenarios in our minds before they happen.

There's a great book on the market called, *Feel the Fear and Do It Anyway*. At some point we have to do just that, or we will find ourselves never taking chances and procrastinating all the time.

I often imagine myself jumping into a pit of fire. I repeat this visualization over and over until I feel a sense of courage. It doesn't matter how many times you jump. Jump in the fire a hundred times if you must, but jump in.

Even seminar leader, Anthony Robbins, works uses the concept of fire to motivate people and conducts a fire walk seminar.

My visualization of jumping into fire really helps me. It can help you, too. If you fear anything, like driving, visualize taking lessons. See yourself changing lanes and merging on the freeway.... taking your driver's test ... and finally driving your friends around.

Do not let fear hold you hostage. What should be feared is not doing anything at all.

What Do You Fear Doing? What can you do to face the fear?

_____

_____

_____

_____

_____

_____

The Art of Hynopsis or Suggestion Therapy

Fear and negative core beliefs often come in a package. It seems once we solve one problem, another one pops up right behind it.

A great website, Permanentchanges.com, offers numerous suggestion therapy cds on various topics such as Creating Wealth, Goals for Success, and Social Confidence. The prices range from $14.95 to $27.95. **Suggestion therapy is a form of self-hypnosis** that helps destroy negative and limiting belief systems and build more resourceful and empowering ones. I highly recommend self-hypnosis. It can provide inspiration and motivation a person needs to transform his or her life.

Find Your Purpose

Have you wondered if you are following the right path?

According to the book, *The Power of Intention*, when we find ourselves wondering what our true purpose in life is, this is our purpose trying to reconnect with us.

Your purpose has more to do, the author says, with how **you feel about what you do than actually what you are doing**. So it boils down to feelings. I think our true purpose also is strongly connected to our childhood dreams. Do you remember what you wanted to be when you grew up?

Other people's expectations for us and the pressures of life can block us or interfere with what we were born to do.

Do yourself a favor and be still. Get back in touch with your inner child. Ask that child what do they want to be when they grow up. Write the dream down right now.

_____
_____
_____
_____

Hobbies May Be Linked to Your Purpose

Do you have a hobby? A hobby is also a tell-tell sign about what your purpose in life might be.

What is your hobby?

_____

How long have you've worked at this hobby?

_____

How many hours per week do you devote to this hobby?

_____

My hobbies have always consumed me. I make time to write, paint, or read at least for three hours two or three days per week. Rate your hobby passion meter below.

My passion for this hobby is super high. Yes/No (circle one)

My passion for this hobby is not as strong as it use to be. Yes/No (circle one)

I would like to find a way to earn a second income with this hobby. Yes/No (circle one)

Are You Ready to Make Something Happen?

Many people never look closely at their business skills they've learned on the job. A person who studied business in school doesn't necessarily know more than a person who did not attend business school. What type of skills have you acquired that will help jump start a small business? Identify your best skill set below so you can become more aware of your new strengths.

_____

_____

_____

_____

_____

The next several exercises will walk you through the steps of a condensed business plan, followed by Invention 101 and Media 101.

Let's start first with writing down three business ideas you think are appropriate under each of the following categories—media, product, and service. The business does not have to be something that is easily recognizable. It can be off-the-wall as long as it interests you and you feel it can serve a need or has an important benefit.

1. What type of business would you love to start that is media oriented?

_____

2. What industry would you like to design a product for?

_____

3. What type of business would you love to start that is service oriented?

_____

4. What is your business name?

_____

Tip: *It's okay to team up with someone who may be better in another area to help you make your dreams take off.*

Business Plan Basics

The business plan is the expected way to communicate your ideas to others in a clear and concise manner. It serves as a prospectus for potential lenders and partners. Business plans explain how the business will function, how it will be financed, and how it will be managed.

Overall, it forces you to take a look at your entire business proposal critically and objectively.

Take a moment to write the mission statement. Explain how this business is going to make a difference. What sets it apart from similar businesses? What does growth look like over the next three years? This is the part of the plan where you can express your passion.

My/Our Mission is:

_____

_____

_____

_____

Decide next on your business organization. You can structure it as a sole proprietorship, LLC, or Corporation.

Tip: Keep expenses down and buy the building where you set up your business.
—D. Bach

Checklist For Business Plans

Parts of the Plan:

Marketing
Sales
Management
Financial

Checklist for Marketing

Who's your customer?
How large is your market?
Is it growing, steady, or decreasing?
Identify direct competitors. Who are they?

Checklist for Sales

What are your products or service?
What media will you use to advertise?
What's your budget?

Quick checklist for Management

Design a chart showing key positions along with duties in the organization
List benefits, compensation, salary, and payroll for first 3 years
Specify management responsibilities
Specify work schedules
Obtain resumes of key personnel

Quick checklist for finances

Start Up Date of Business
List your overhead
Prepare monthly Cash Flow statements
(shows flow of cash in and out of business)
P& L Statement
Determine if you will use a fiscal or calendar year

Invention 101

If you are an imaginative person you can probably design a new product or improve one that already exist.

Here is an easy way to get started. It's so easy a child can do it. Think of two things that work together like a broom and dust pan or toothpaste and a toothbrush.

Next, draw several different ways they can work together as one gadget. I remember a product I saw on television several years ago. Someone designed a dog brush in the shape of a hand mitten. What can you think of? Jot down two ideas.

Product One:_____

Product Two:_____

How can these work together? Draw it on a piece of paper.

Product One:_____

Product Two:_____

How can these work together? Draw it on a piece of paper.

Media 101

This exercise is similar to Invention 101. If you have always dreamed of busting into the media, now is the time. I want you to create a synopsis for your show, video or TV/Movie idea. It cannot be more than three sentences. Many screenwriters pitch their ideas in the form of a synopsis. **This is the perfect way to present any idea because it's precise and to the point.** No one wants to hear a long, zigzag, to the left, then to the right, over the mountain, down in the valley, etc. story. You get my drift?? You have to know your story before you can convey it to others. However, don't give away the ending. You have to learn to entice or tease, so people will want to hear more. Here's an example synopsis based on a family movie/theatre drama I wrote years ago called *Little Italy*.

Logline: *Family story about a half breed girl growing up in the eighties who has a love/hate relationship with three of the neighborhood "guidos" living across the street from her house.*

Write down your synopsis here:

_____
_____
_____
_____
_____

If you're not interested in writing a treatment or synopsis for a movie, maybe consider developing an online magazine, TV hosting, producing a radio or video show, syndicate a comic strip, market a cd, or write a book.

These are sure fire ways to earn income while you sleep. Work smart. The average nine to five job will not build riches. One must have two or three projects in the bag that will help triple or quadruple ones net worth, leading to financial independence and security.

My Story

"Understand your mission is to make history while you're here"

—Nas

Before I wrap up this book, I would like to take a moment to share my story with you. I want you to know where I come from and what gave me the power or juice to write this book. Shall we walk down memory lane together?

I was born in San Francisco, California and was raised by a single parent along with three other siblings. We lived in a very multicultural section of a small city next to SF called Daly City. Mother made sure we attended catholic schools from grades one through twelve so we could get the best education possible. Because she strongly detested raising children in apartments, she purchased a three bedroom, two bathroom colonial style house in the early 1970's, a home where we could be comfortable and run free the way children should. Our house was located on Hanover Street, the most vibrant block in the area. There were always ten or thirteen kids to play with from sun up to sun down.

It seems all my life I have been a ball of energy. I was a hyper child who knew she wanted to work as an artist around the age of four or five. I possessed advance drawing skills as a youngster, had to deal with grown up responsibilities before graduating from high school, and was approached many times with acting and modeling opportunities while on the verge of illiteracy. Each of these issues overlapped other, causing me to feel like I was trapped in chaos.

They also played a major role in causing my life to "splinter" due too many choices and pressure, making me lose sight of my life purpose.

My sister and I shared a bedroom where magical things happened every day. Our imaginations transformed our bedroom into white table restaurants and barbie doll cities. My skills in art lured the attention of family, friends, and teachers who encouraged me to pursue the arts. Drawing was all I really wanted to do. Art became an obsession in a sense. While other kids in class were busy doing the alphabet, I was busy in the back of the room reproducing pictures of the Last Super.

When my mother learned I was falling behind in reading comprehension, she became extremely angry and took matters into her own hands. To keep me in line and make sure I could read, she forced me to sit next to her bedside and read a chapter from a book she selected every night. No child of hers was going to be illiterate. My mother stressed the importance of education almost daily. She was an avid reader herself. Mom could read a five hundred page Jackie Collin's book in two nights and she never missed an issue of the San Francisco Chronicle. She told me once she began reading the newspaper at the age of three.

I must say, reading the newspaper at the age of three was quite impressive, but it wasn't enough to make me enjoy reading. Reading, in my eyes, was like a death sentence. Sometimes I would get so frustrated that I'd skip a page or two. I remember thinking I had her fooled. In the end, however, the only person I hurt was myself. When I took the required entry exam administered by The Sisters of Presentation High School, my reading level was below my grade level. This time I was forced to enroll in a special reading lab course. I was going to read whether I liked it or not. It was my last chance to get it right.

My instructor, Mrs. Weiss, made us read *The House of Mirth* and *Romeo and Juliet*, write book reports, and short stories. We even had to review Phonics. By the end of my ninth grade year I shot up to eleventh grade reading and comprehension. My most dreaded class became the most celebrated. Suddenly books were very cool to me and I loved to write. Now I had three hobbies—art, reading, and creative writing which naturally lead to working as an ESL Tutor when I transferred to City College of San Francisco where I declared the Cinematic Arts with a concentration in Screenwriting as my major.

Aside from all my defeats and victories in education, there was another side to my life that involved fashion modeling. Many people thought I should pursue modeling and I had several offers from agencies and from a friend who had contacts at *Seventeen* Magazines.

Everyone had a plan for my future. I was pulled in many directions. I was enticed by the modeling world yet was determined to work behind the scenes as a screenwriter. One of my girlfriends, Michelle, was embarking on a career in acting at the time I was dealing with issues of making it big in Hollywood. Together we set out to conquer it.

I don't want to bore you with all the details. Michelle worked in theatre and as an extra on The Prince of Bel Air. We managed to go to celebrity events. Hollywood was not what we thought it was. No one took my scripts seriously, but they tried to push me into acting which was not my forte. It didn't take long for me to move back home, get back into school, and rethink my career choice.

I visited Los Angeles whenever I got a chance. Michelle stayed in Hollywood for nearly ten years. Filmmaking was put on hold as I started to evolve more spiritually. I also started to entertain thoughts of having my own business which took me down a whole new road. The problem I had was deciding on the type of business I wanted.

In 1997 I enrolled in a Small Business Certificate Program which led me to research the pros and cons of several business ventures I was interested in. The one I wanted the most, the one I was most committed to, was publishing my art. Unfortunately the business crashed and burned behind a shady art rep who approached me, offering his services for two years. During those two years he was suppose to find a licensing agreement for my art, but he ended up putting little effort into securing a contract. Mind you, he was paid $3,800 up front. One thing I learned is **never give anyone their entire fee up front**. I felt he got lazy after he got paid, and there I was out of money with two years down the drain.

Eventually, after trial and error, I settled on being an infopreneur entrepreneur. Writing is one of several things I feel I have the most control over. I see myself writing books, recording cds, videos, and business kits during the years to come.

Afterword

I would like to take a moment to thank you for supporting my book. I dedicate it to ordinary people who want to improve their lives and provide for themselves and their families.

I invite your comments and any suggestions to add to the next edition of this book in the future. If you would like to receive information about business kits and books published by IWS since 1967 or referral for MMA Software and/or an excellent source for Courtesy Deposits, send me an email.

Send emails to daphnekm@lycos.com

Again, I hope you have not only learned something new, but feel you can actually put into action without much difficulty these tips, strategies, and insight today.

The sooner you start, the sooner you'll be on your way to accomplishing your financial goals.

Good luck and peace to all.…

Special Note*

This book is available to sell as a premium offer to your clients of your business and for use at seminars in loose-leaf binder format. Please contact the author via email in regards to prices on premium orders and seminar/workshop events.

Book orders are can be placed through Iuniverse.com, Amazon.com, and Barnes and Noble. Com.

Appendix

Investments Clubs

In the past investment clubs were extremely private and accessible to men who were rich. Now they are open to both males and females and people of all races and religions.

Investment clubs are made up of a network of investors, experts, and entrepreneurs to exchange investment opportunities, knowledge, strategies, and resources.

There are two investment clubs I think are worth mentioning.

1. NREI, National Real Estate Investment Club, specializes in Real Estate, online classes, webinars, meetings, mixers, member cruises, exclusive member only investment opportunities and more.

Visit nreiclub.com for information on how to join.

"Great profits in the company of good friends"

2. This is the slogan of The Oxford Club, a low profile club that focuses on stocks. The club is uniquely modeled after the old English Gentlemen's clubs that were popular during the 19th century.

They have been very successful at predicting trends and directing their members to opportunities that have produced gains as high as 906%.

The Oxford Club currently has 65,000 members all over the globe.

Below are some of the benefits you will receive as a member:

1. Bimonthly *Communique*: gives recommendations on investments to watch for, techniques to help you become a more knowledgeable investor, insights from market experts, traders, and company insiders. There is also a special page called "What To Do With Your Money Today," highlighting investments that members can profit from most.

2. *OC Club Edition*, a newsletter to keep members posted on club events, meetings, financial news, and miscellaneous features like selling and buying real estate, legal advice, etc.

3. Exclusive White Paper Reports with immediate news concerning issues that may threaten member's wealth.

4. Urgent Investor Briefings: covering a new profit opportunity that cannot wait.

5. Member Services Liaison

6. Members-Only Discount Brokerage and Investment Services

7. Members-Only Discounts on products and services

8. Profiteering Expeditions

Visit www.oxfordclub.com for more information.

Tip: Gold is on the rise and may be a good investment to look into. Remember there are two types of gold: rare coins which people collect and bullion which is sold and bought actively on the market.

Recommended Reading and Websites

<u>Self Help and Motivational Books:</u>

Life Strategies, Dr. Phil
The Art of The Deal, Donald Trump
You're Hired, Bill Rancic
The Law of Attraction, Michael Losier
Rich Dad/Poor Dad, Robert T. Kiyosaki
Unlimited Power, Anthony Robbins
How To Make Big Money In Real Estate, Tyler Hicks
The Automatic Millionaire, David Bach
Go It Alone, Bruce Judson

<u>Spiritual Books:</u>

The Power of Intention, Dr. Wayne Dyer
The Four Agreements, Don Miguel Ruiz
The Power of Now, Eckhart Tolle
The Five Enemies, Daphne K. McCorery

<u>Websites:</u>

Inc-it-Now.com
Sba.gov/
USChamber.Org
Franshisegator.Com
Directinvesting.com

Ingdirect.com
Entrepreneur.Com
E*trade.Com
Vistaprint.Com
Womensinitiative.org

<u>TV Shows:</u>

The Big Idea
Mad Money
High Net Worth
The Millionaire Inside
Flip This House

978-0-595-46442-5
0-595-46442-4